Blippi

Let's See Animals!

SCHOLASTIC

We're going to visit animals!

Come on, let's go!

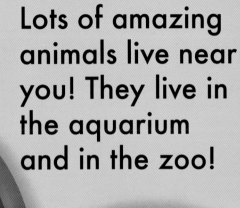

Lots of amazing animals live near you! They live in the aquarium and in the zoo!

A strong hard shell

Legs like flippers

Turtles can stay under water
for about five hours.
That's a really long time!

Lettuce for lunch!

No teeth

Wow! A turtle is so interesting!

Back fin

Tail fin

More fins!

Check this out! It's a shark! Sharks have lots of fins to help them move through the water.

There are some really big fish in here!

Fin that helps with steering

Gills for breathing

A stingray is flat and sleek and has a really long tail!

Very sharp tail

Fin

Eyes

Wowee! Sea creatures you're allowed to touch!

Snail

Starfish

Sea urchin

Penguins are birds that don't fly!

Pointy beak for catching fish

Penguins waddle when they walk. Can you waddle like a penguin?

Webbed feet for paddling in water

**Wings like
flippers**

Female
duck

Ducks say "Quack!"
Can you quack
like a duck?

Male
duck

Webbed
feet

14

Ducks are
so, so, so
cute!

15

Whoa! Look at what it is! It's a polar bear! See his big paws? They help him walk on snow and ice.

Great sense of smell!

Thick fur for staying warm

Big paws

Hey, meerkats sure are fun to watch at the zoo! Up to 50 meerkats can live together in one group.

18

A group of meerkats is called a mob. Meerkats take turns looking out for danger.

On hind legs to see better

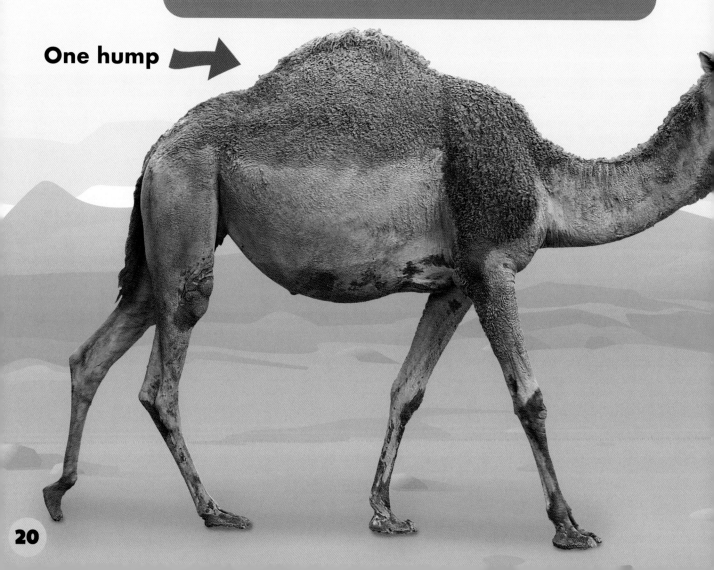

Two toes

Orange fur – my favourite!

No two tigers have the same exact stripes!

Very sharp teeth

Wow! That's a REALLY big kitty cat! The tiger is the biggest kind of cat in the world.

Thanks for exploring amazing animals with me!

Now can you fill this page with stickers of your favourite animals?

© 2021 Kideo, Inc.

© 2021 Kideo, Inc.

© 2021 Kideo, Inc.